The Odyssey Of A Lady

E. H. Kinyon

DEDICATED TO BESSIE

I am proud to say I was part of her crew from May 3, 1941 till August 18, 1945.

E. H. Kinyon

CONTENTS

ACKNOWLEDGMENTS

All those who were essential in bringing this story back to life: Esther Palmer (formerly Kinyon), Lezlie Kinyon, Gary R. Boodhoo, Curtis Clark, Bud Whitmore, Bob LeBeau, everyone who emailed asking when this was finally getting published, and, most importantly, all those who bravely served aboard the USS Talbot DD114/APD-7.

- Thea A. Kinyon Boodhoo

INTRODUCTION

The fate of the USS Talbot DD114/APD-7 is told in the Epilogue, but the fate of the author is not. My grandfather, Ellis Holden Kinyon, or Kinny as his friends and family knew him, was lost in a sudden storm while sailing in Puget Sound with his son David in 1958. He was a mystery to me growing up - a grandfather I'd been cheated out of ever meeting, and for my mother, Lezlie, he was a father she remembered only from pictures and stories.

I first read *The Odyssey Of A Lady* when I was sixteen. That was ten years, almost to the day, before I pulled it back out of an old box to transcribe it, and almost fourteen years ago as I write this. On my first read, as an aspiring writer, I found it wordy and offensive, but also creative, and I dreamed of someday re-writing it into something "marketable", without really knowing what that meant.

I was also disappointed that the story was more about the ship than about the man. His life was what I wanted to know about, not the war he fought in. Certainly not some boat. After all, it was a boat that robbed me of knowing him in the first place.

Since then, I've learned more about him. There are the stories I've heard from my grandmother of course, and I was lucky to make it to the last APD 4-Stack Veteran's Reunion where I got to meet some of the surviving crewmembers of the Talbot, who made me feel very welcome when I didn't know anyone there. (You can read more about the reunion at the blog that accompanies this book: the-odyssey-of-a-lady.tumblr.com.) I can't thank them enough for the time and courtesy they gave me, especially Curtis Clark, Bud Whitmore and Bob LeBeau.

There are photographs, as well – lots of them. Last year, I scanned a huge collection of old 35mm slides that my grandmother had kept in a cupboard for decades. (You can see them at kinyonslides.tumblr.com.) From those, I know they took road trips to Yellowstone, vacationed on Hick's Lake, and drove a powder blue 4-door. I know the grinning faces of their friends at the base in Bettles Field, Alaska, where Kinny was stationed right after he married my grandmother, and I know that they liked to have everyone over for card games and beers. I know that Kinny started building an add-on to their house after they moved back to Washington State, and I know that it was never finished.

Kinny was a short, thin man, with a witty, slapstick sense of humor, and always in motion. He drank, smoked, and smiled a lot. My grandmother remembers him most fondly for his belief in education. He told her once: "You are going back to school. You are fine now, but when we get old we will have nothing to talk about." He had a precise way of speaking and didn't waste words.

She always tells me he gave her "the learning bug" - an addiction to knowledge that she passed on to my mother and myself.

Another thing changed between the first time I read *The Odyssey Of A Lady* and the second time, a decade later. I went to work as a writer, in the advertising industry. I learned to find the unique and special things about a product, and sell those, flaws and all, because in a world of hand waving and overpromising, it's the genuine that stands out. When I read this story again through that lens, I saw its incredible character: zealous, charming, unique, and, like my grandfather, filled with life and character. I no longer felt compelled to re-write it, and realized that even if I tried I couldn't do any better than he did.

That said, the story was written on typewriter in a small room on a warship, with storms and bombs and danger lurking around every island, so it was pretty far from perfect when I picked it up. Some parts were barely legible, and pages were missing. As I transcribed the photocopies of the original that my grandma mailed me, I had to make some edits, correcting spelling and grammatical errors, and smoothing out a sentence here and there. The story and the style are unchanged.

I also chose, after four years of deliberation, not to censor the blatant racism. Whatever else *The Odyssey of A Lady* is, it's a piece of history, and as history I believe it should remain intact. I hope you are offended, as I was, when you read some of the words he chose, but I hope that doesn't stop you from reading.

If you love adventure or history, especially naval history, get excited because you're about to read an utterly unique account of World War II, written from the perspective of a warship bent on revenge and eager for excitement on the high seas.

If you served, or have ever cared about someone who served, whether you knew them personally or just, like me, wish you had, then this edition is dedicated to you. I hope you enjoy it.

And if you're just curious, well, Kinny probably would've said that's the best thing there is to be. Never stop.

- Thea Kinyon Boodhoo

E. H. Kinyon

FORWARD

I would have made this story more complete, but due to limitations of both time and accurate material, it would have been impossible.

The whole story has by no means been told. Just the highlights have been here in described.

Here is hoping that it will prove interesting to any or all persons that may be plagued with the task of trying to decipher the following text.

E. H. Kinyon

When I first saw her, she was nestled among others of her kind at the side of the long dock at the Destroyer Base in San Diego. I decided that even if she were some years older than I, there was a chance that duty aboard her would be good, so I put in my chit for transfer. My luck was good (or bad as the case may be) and soon we were making our way to sea. I found most of my time being spent at the rail at first, but things soon smoothed out.

I'd like to set down a few facts about her, as I have seen her in the past five years. She has been a good girl most of the time, but once in a while she gets just plain and simple NASTY. She is small as ships go nowadays, only a little over three hundred feet long and is very narrow for her length. This makes her fall enormously in a very small swell, especially if it comes up on either side of her flanks. This is cause for much discomfort to her crew. Very near retirement age, she knows not the word "quit" and so she still seductively undulates her slight, twenty-eight year old frame from port to port. She has more power than a hundred automobile engines nestling nicely in her gizzard and her brains are generally good. At times she can neither see nor hear. Then she must feel her way along, but she doesn't mind this at all - rather, she glories in it. She is an altruist, enjoying herself and kicking about like a young colt. In spite of her contrariness and meanness, she has been home (or what have you) for quite a few men.

Beyond that year I spent on her before the war, her past is shrouded in mystery. She seems to remember happy days around the Hawaiian Islands and has been in almost every navy yard in the United States. She seems to recollect dimly of rollicking days on the East Bank of the Atlantic, but these have become disjointed over the passing years.

My first sight of her was in the quiet year of 1941 and the even quieter year of May. She was then attached to the anti-submarine Warfare School at San Diego. More than a year was to pass before her role in the new war.

I shall skip briefly over those uneventful days in her routine work around San Diego, saying that she was much like a workhorse that had been well broken to the plow. Even then she showed that she resented the well established. At times she would gambol about and flirt her well-shaped little stern in a very unaccountable manner. Perhaps memories would tickle her fancy at these times.

Her future then held promise of nothing more than an occasional storm or maybe an unsuspected reef. Sure she could never do much in the Great Storm that she may have felt approaching, she was almost broken in spirit, but sleeping deep within her ageing soul was a spark that would forever make her a very real and living thing in the hearts of her shipmates.

Then came the war. "The Japs have bombed Pearl Harbor," they said. "Hunt for enemy ships to the west and south of Point Loma." She was off. She was like a hunting dog straining at the leash. But all she did was hunt.

That night she made her way back to anchorage. Age seemed to hang on her that night. Never the less, she began packing her bag for a hectic journey, discarding this and rearranging that until she was flushed with excitement like a young girl on her honeymoon. From the way she acted, one would have thought she was just being commissioned, never guessing her to be one of the respectable old ladies of the fleet.

The next day she was up to her neck in work. But did she mind? Rather not, she flung herself into it as though she had to prove herself not only willing, but more than able.

She was told to chaperone the Saratoga to Pearl Harbor. Later word of the Sara explained how she had scared Hell out of the Japs who were in the Marshalls at the time.

Her heroic efforts to take Sara to Pearl will long be remembered by the men she lived with at the time. Bouncing and rolling as if she couldn't get out with her friend Sara fast enough.

Then she found that Sara would want bigger and faster girls with her on the big trip. Her full contrariness showed her disappointment. She was stubborn and mean. All hands knew that she resented being taken from the chase. We could all feel that she was just being mean to show how deeply she was hurt.

At the thought of Pearl, she wept. Her shipmates had been hurt. Some of them were dead. Here was the Oklahoma and the Arizona, who would never again know the lift and swell of the sea. Many others were mortally wounded. Never again would the sea hiss and roll before their feet. Others, not so grievously hurt, would some day pay due respect to the villains and their assassinism. She vowed vengeance on the Yellow People. She would devote her life to this end.

The Admiral mistakenly thought she would rather sleep her days out in a quiet home. So he sent her back to Diego to train more anti-sub men.

Her voyage home was more than she wanted to bear. She rankled and burned in a heavy sea. The combination struck terror in the men she had coddled in the smooth waters of southern California. She was furiously planning with an eye to the future.

I will always think that somehow she was the cause of it, but of course I shall never know. Somehow, she wriggled out of the boresome duties of a school ship.

Her next home was San Francisco. Here at least, she could see could see that the rest of them got off to a good start. For almost four months she idled around Frisco like a worn out hunting dog. She kept longing watch on those going out and eagerly sped out to welcome those who had made the voyage. Those who were limping back, she carefully helped in under the bridge. The proud she met like a puppy, fawning on their heels.

The activity was exciting, but turned to ashes at the first bite. In all, she was dissatisfied and longing for the hunt.

On a bright day in the latter part of May, 1942, she was once again called. She raced to be of service, and was hastily armed with some of the new-fangled anti-aircraft automatics. Her obsolete guns were shined and polished. Again her bags were packed and she waited.

Soon she was off, herding three submarines like a collie with sheep. Her nose and ears buried deeply in the water, keeping a lead to the north. Her conscience may have hurt her for not saying goodbye to her friends, but not enough to show. She was on the trail, holding up her honor and not about to let anyone think she was a worthless old lady.

She made it into Seattle in less than a week, and was off again after a hasty drink of firewater, intoxicated with the prospect of keeping the honor of her kind. She knew the Japs wanted Alaska, and she wasn't going to let them have it.

The Sea and the Wind prove every ship that sails around the islands of the north, testing each venturesome being to see just what it can take. Legend has it, that no storm will ever be worse than the one initiating a newcomer into their realm. They made no exception for the Lady.

It was in the narrow straits called Akutan Pass, one day out of Dutch Harbor, that the furies unleashed their weight and might. Down from the north, as the current changed in that direction, came a williwaw. The ocean protested with all its might that a puny thing like the wind could ever change its course. It reached up in defiance for the screeching hurricane that trod on its toes. The Lady, trapped between the devil and the sea, lurched, groaned and shuddered under tons of water crashing down upon her unprotected back. Her sturdy frame was at times completely submerged, the water swirling madly around her decks. How the water could be so bad was beyond her poor mind. She didn't know she was undergoing the test.

For forty minutes she shouldered her way through that cursed strait. For forty minutes she wondered at the water standing vertical instead of as it should–the spray that slanted either up or down at its seeming will, that seemed so slight, but was as a solid wall when encountered.

The water suddenly smoothed off as with a trowel. The wind died down. She had made her way through the narrow corridor, and the results were as incongruous as an oyster in a flowerpot. She had passed the test. Legend has since proved true. The initiation to the realm of the Silver One was the worst storm she ever saw. Never again has she had to battle her way through the unshackled giants as she did that day. She had proved her mettle. The giants were satisfied.

That evening she dove into Dutch Harbor and set her anchor into the bottom of the bay. Patiently she waited for another spirit-lifting drink. She would then be ready for anything that could happen. This was the second of June 1942.

Lordy, how patiently she stood waiting that night, expecting the Japs to show their teeth at any time. She was ready to shove them down their throats.

The morning broke at the unearthly hour of 4 A.M. and with it came the Little Yellow Devils. At the dock, where she was being delivered her shot, she strained at the restraining lines, her miniature anti-aircraft potting at any likely target, while all the time she knew that her spirit (high as it was) was not enough. So like the lady she was, she shook herself of the remains of the bomb-wrecked dock and her lines. She flirted her slim stern into a fog cover outside the bay.

She slunk around the island and regally let herself into a little bay designated as the hideout for her and a few others who weren't going to let the Slant-Eyed Sons of the Sun of Heaven have our Alaska.

She was rankled, and we all knew it, despite how she feigned indifference. Her sisters in Pearl would have to wait for Vengeance while she supped at the bitter dish of disappointment.

She shuddered in the very marrow of her finely formed frame. Her heart was breaking and she determined never to let the Japs have her land. She was ready at any time to sacrifice herself to the noble cause for which she had suffered this ignoble defeat.

Her life became devoted to the cause for which she fought (or rather, waited). Her depth charges were set minimum in case the Japs were to attempt to land. Her torpedoes were gleaming and labeled for delivery to likely targets of the Jap fleet. She preferred a carrier, but would take anything that offered itself if the case should come up. Her horses were ready to surge her through the icy northern seas to protect her homeland at this bastion of the Storm King.

Her disdain of the odds was remarkable. If she were to die now, her death would be honorable. She would go down as a Fighting Lady and not as one of those who had chosen the painless suicide of decommissioning. She would prove her worth and her virtue. Her destiny would have been fulfilled.

Her heart eventually quieted down and she re-joined the many. She took pride in doing a job that only a few were helping her with: supplying this bulwark of her home.

She was a sensitive one, leaping in the foam and basking in the occasional sun - sun that brought homesickness to heart for the sunny lands she had left far to the south. Yet she exalted in the survey of lands that she had never seen before. She had developed an insatiable appetite for the unknown. She was an adventuress. Here is the thing that ranks first in the list of what she likes to do best.

Her missions took her into unlikely ports. She rolled in the treacherous seas off the islands of Kodiak, Atka, and Unalaska. Kodiak was her temporary home. Later she shifted to another as cold and hard as her sturdy sides. She seemed to love Dutch Harbor with its harsh, tall mountains, which looked as if the slightest shove would send them falling into the bay.

She nosed her way into Cooks Inlet and thrilled at the wondrous sight of the invisible sun tinting the harsh mountains in the distance, with magic brush, in pink and gold and other make-believe colors. She rested a time at Anchorage, making friends and looking over the white crags that overlooked the bay.

Wearying of her play, she ran away again to Seward. She didn't quite know what to make of the wild, dense undergrowth that overhung the little basin in which she stood.

Alas, she couldn't escape her work, and once more she was called to do her bit.

Her lover was the cold north wind, which swept down from the frozen and mysterious northland. She would stand there powdering her nose in the little bay at Dutch Harbor. Then the cold wind would caress her with its icy fingers. She would shudder, as a lady should.

Fascinated by his whispered promises, she was lured away to his home. It was late July. She took a northern course from Dutch Harbor and frisked gaily through the tippled waters of the Bering Sea to the home of her beloved, whispering her hopes to the waves. They were blank in their answers. They had seen others on this self same trip.

As the warm Alaska sun bathed her journey, her thoughts increasingly turned to her home in the sunny south. She continued to Nome, but soon lost heart. For several days, off the bleak land of the north, she reconnoitered her thoughts. Then, not hearing from her lover, she decided she had made a mistake. She rested, admiring the quiet, blue-gold scenery of Nome. Then she made up her mind to hike herself back to lands she knew.

The midnight sun amazed her, but the ever-present threat of locking ice was enough to throw any freedom-loving lady into a panic. After collecting a couple of souvenirs - svelte northern furs and trinkets of walrus ivory - she hastened to the south, secretly ashamed of the fool she had made of herself by wooing the harsh north wind.

In familiar waters, she heard of an expedition being made to the west, further than she had ever been before. She scurried to go along. Work was her lot and exclusiveness was not to be had this time. Her job among the many was herding perhaps the strangest expedition that ever sailed the icy seas.

The herd was composed of many barges and stranger craft, the strangest of all being a spirit shackled in ignominious defeat to a vessel that towed her along. She was loaded heavily with TNT and other choice tidbits. Through the rolling swells, she once had signatured, with the breath of heaven in her great wings. Nothing remained now, except the stark skeletons of her fingers that thrust themselves into heaven, imploring the same heaven to let her once again be as her sisters, who were on their own. Our Lady, seeing her as she feared others might see her someday, discreetly stood on the other side of the mass and quietly did her job.

Finally they reached Adak, a new base for her to live. Here at last were new lands to conquer.

In her eagerness, she stubbed her toe on a nasty boulder that rested too near the surface to be ignored. She ranted and raved on her way back to Dutch Harbor. She knew that she had pulled a boner that would be noted in her record with disgrace. She could only lick her wound. Showing her contrariness, she floundered her after parts in the ocean swell, as if by sheer force she could mend the hurt and go back into the fray, but her lot was hospitalization. Again the Leering Jap had slipped away from her. She renewed her vow of vengeance, and limped her painful way back to Seattle to have her locomotive parts repaired.

She was happy to find that in ten days she would be ready to go again; and so she was. Again, adventure lured her to the north.

This time, however, she was doomed to ever pass the time like the ship upon which the Ancient Mariner sailed forever the seas. For weary months she schooned and scudded, sliced and slugged her way through the wild ocean of that land. Until at

[Editor's note: pages 10 and 11 of the typewritten copy that this was transcribed from were missing at the time of publication.]

The day before she left the yard; one of her sisters sidled close after a weary trip to where the Lady was to go. Her excited whisperings went on and on through the night. She was finding out some pointers on how she should act now that she was changed.

Her men came back to man her again that night, and both were ready to go.

GETTING ACQUAINTED

The normally brown hills of Vallejo were lush and green in springtime splendor as we sailed late in April of 1943 bound for Pearl Harbor. From there we did not know, but she, being of the sect, knew that adventure was calling to her with a loud voice.

She took to the swells with a slightly different roll than she had before, daintily spurning the heavy ones with her foot. She always was a lady.

In company with another of the class now known as APDs (high-speed transports), she tripped her way to Pearl. Her growing excitement was a wonder to behold. She became vain but not so as to overshadow the fact that she was still a lady.

Upon arrival in Pearl, she decided that she must have adjustments made to her new clothes. Since she was beginning a new life, she must also look different. Her vanity is the only explanation for the hideous green she used for a long time after when she rouged her cheeks.

Now she deemed herself quite ready. She pointed her sleek nose into the deep green swells of the semi-tropic sea and glided south for several days, lost in thoughts and plans for her new life. She was happy. And at last, she was free.

But what was this? A green head appeared over the rail. King Neptune had come aboard to hold his court.

Brave men quivered in their boots, but Neptunus, seeing the Lady was an old friend, let her off easy. He crowned and christened each man aboard her a Trusty Shellback, the hateful name of Pollywog forever discarded.

[Editor's note: pages 14 and 15 of the typewritten copy that this was transcribed from were missing at the time of publication.]

She was satisfied now, after seeing these happy people, with their shiny teeth flashing friendly smiles and their happy laughter. Early the next morning, she left–but not without regrets, for she would never find another port as nice as Nukalofa. Part of her memory would always enshrine the recollections of the little jungle Kingdom with the Queen who had outlived 5 husbands. She vowed that if the occasion would ever come again someday, she would return to pay her respects to a truly lovely tropical island.

But she hadn't come to play. She had come for the vengeance that still lay heavy on her heart - to make the Nips pay for her sisters that lay on the bottom of Pearl Harbor. Duty called her again and she was ready and willing to go.

The Japs had their subs strung along the shipping lanes to Australia, and she was to escort a small convoy to Townsville. It was small stuff, not the big time she had come for, but just the same, she slithered through the Coral Sea and around the Great Barrier Reef with her charges.

She was touchy about the waters inside the reef and careful through the treacherous shoals and shallows until they were safely ensconced within the red brick breakwater of Townsville. She was anxious to go and didn't stay long.

Back to Noumea, then she was off again. This time, she would taste the fruit of vengeance with a small convoy to

Guadalcanal. She sized up her future home: blue mountains, palms, hot humid atmosphere and fantastic sunsets. Past Savo Island, she could see Tulagi in the distance. This would be a wonderful place to begin her work against the Japs, but it was back to Noumea for a little while until her home was ready. She didn't want to see the show until the lights were out.

After a quick vacation in Auckland, New Zealand, she heard that things were happening to her liking up in the Solomons.

Up to this time, she had been largely a guide and shepherd. Now she was on her own. If any escorting was done, she would be the one escorted - as Hell on wheels to the Japs. Vengeance would be had, and she was determined to be the tool.

No longer a gamboling girl, carefree as the wind, her duties weighed heavily on her.

She took a side trip to New Hebrides. Since her guests that time were Seabees, she dropped them the first chance she got. They were nice fellows, but not the kind she wanted in her work.

Finally, her new home. Across Iron Bottom Bay, through a little passage, into a quiet, and very pretty, little cove between North and South Florida Islands, is a little bay seemingly designed for hiding out and virtually invisible from the air. Its jungle-littered boundaries and deep blue waters captivated her from the very beginning.

She didn't seem to mind the intense jungle heat that was so oppressive to her crew. She just seemed to ignore it.

It was here that she let others in on the secret of her work. How she gloried in telling of her plans to take the ill-gotten gains of the Japs in the only way she could - carrying men and equipment to assault the enemy-held territories under the cover of darkness, with the night and her speed to supplement the guns she carried. The date was June 26, 1943.

LIFE IN THE SOLOMONS

On the 28th of June, 1943, she was given orders to go to Guadalcanal. She waited awhile at Lugna Point while her captain went ashore for her orders. Next, to Russell Islands, just wrestled from the Japs, where she embarked her fighting guests. They were the first of a long line.

The afternoon of June 29th, she was on her first mission. Imagine her feeling of indignation when she found she had to drag a little sister along behind her. Yes, following her like a little tag-a-long was a jeep lighter, to help her when she got to her destination. She handled this indignity at once; beating, drowning, and casting it away. I suppose many times big brothers and sisters have felt the same way, but never have I seen this done - and with such dispatch and efficiency! At least the equipment in the lighter was replaceable.

All that night she steamed through the Jap hell islands. Rendova and New Georgia surrounded her. She quietly felt her way up the Blanche Channel (The Slot) until she was opposite her destination.

She crept quietly through those waters, almost totally blind and land locked, with no room for high-speed escape tactics. She was as nervous as a colt, passing well within rifle shot of these dark sinister islands - land that seemed to peer at her through evil, slanting eyes.

At any moment she expected an attack from any quarter. Pitfalls uncharted in her guidebook - reefs and a multitude of other dangers - made the way difficult. But on she went.

She heaved a little sigh as she made the final flirt of her little stern and stood in the peaceful bay at Oniavisi. The darkness and heat engulfed her. It was the sort of awful quiet one would expect while smothered in a closet.

She put the Dead-End-Kids in the water and told them to take her guests to the beach. They were eager to proceed.

The night was perspiring down the backs of the troops as they moved in on the little beachhead. The Dead End Kids were rowdy playing in the unknown darkness, but nothing stirred on that forbidding shape ahead. The first of them reached the shore, and uneventfully walked to dry land. A shallow victory, but gratefully accepted.

It was getting light now, and faint stirrings could be seen on the island as our boys crept through the foliage. It was raining just a little harder now. An unnatural chill made teeth chatter in the morning heat. It was still very quiet.

Suddenly a shot, then several more. A little Filipino fellow was settling his own private score. He had spotted a Jap hiding in a tree ready to play sniper. He would play no more.

Word was received that the Lady's sister, who had accompanied her on the trip, was aground. The Lady tried to pull her off. Lines snapped like threads as she tried to loosen the hold the bottom had on her. She called for help, saying she would stand by her sister in case the Jap came by air.

Across the channel on Rendova, bigger ships were now arriving. She could see them moving back and forth, up and down, making themselves hard targets for the Japs.

The Lady's sister was finally freed of the stranglehold late in the morning, but she would have to be towed home. The mighty midget who had pulled her off would do the towing. The Lady still stood by, knowing Mr. Nip was in the air and only about 10 miles away.

She took her stand just behind her hurt sister to help her when the Japs came in.

All hell broke loose as the Japs hit the formation in the shipping area. They had every type of plane that the then-powerful field of Munda could offer.

On they came, first on one side and then the other. The Lady would shift to meet them as they came in for the easy-looking kill below. She met them weaving side-to-side, cross-stitching her sisters' wake.

She and her sisters' guns blazed. The sky was raining fire as Jap planes fell all over the shipping area. Long streams of smoke trailed in the still air like streamers of confetti. A plane broke through after our air cover fighters had hit it, and swirled towards the Lady. But she was no emergency landing field. She slapped it down. Another came up on her ticklish flank. Her anti-aircraft fire quickly hemmed it in, and it splashed in a great silver geyser, backlit by the bright morning sun. A rainbow drifted away. (The soul of a Jap? No Jap has a soul that color.)

Another Jap decided the Lady's impunity was too much for him. He would get her or die in the attempt. He swung around her slim stern amidst a hail of small fire. He dodged as she denied his attentions. He was in front of her. Lazily he swung to attack her, as no lady should be approached. The evil gleam in his eye infuriated her. She reached out with one of her new guns and smashed him right in the face, as one would squash a fly with a swatter. HE DIED.

Now the Lady and her charge were free. They raced south as fast as they could go. Two of her men were hurt, but she considered herself lucky.

She purred to herself the rest of the trip, chortling and

playing as she always does when she is pleased. She was tired and needed rest, but the thought that she had finally done something to avenge her helpless sisters at the bottom of Pearl Harbor kept her in a very good mood.

She rested for a short time at Guadalcanal, but in a couple of days she was ready to go again.

On the second of August, she again had guests. The boys were to make a frontal attack on New Georgia Island, aiding the attack on Munda Air Field by striking the enemy from behind.

After she had received her guests she was again the Lady-of-the-Night. She had five sisters with her this time, all with guests. A big sister screened and a couple cruisers were there to help them all.

All that day she and her sisters steamed up north and around the eastern end of the southern tip of New Georgia. Along the east bank they scuttled like clouds, silent and after sunset, grim and dark.

The night was black, designed for the job ahead. A high cloud obscured the stars and what was left of the moon. It was a good sign. Even the heavens were working against the fiends.

Just after midnight, the Lady and her friends watched the cruisers stirring up the hornets' nest. She was uneasy, but took it in stride. A couple of hours later she and her friends entered Kula Gulf.

She and her sisters formed in lines about 3000 yards off shore. Her big sisters were a little further out and the cruisers stood guard at the door.

She stood patiently in her stall while the boys Higgins made numerous trips to the beach and back with men and supplies that they would need in their fight on the beach.

The Nips kept up a continual barrage of artillery, trying to spot us with star shells. Of course we were quite invisible from the beach, but other types of shells were plunking very close aboard.

As she lay alert in her special stall, she kept notice of

the conflagration all about. Behind her lay Kolombangara. A high, almost circular island infested with Japanese planes and artillery. In front of her lay Rice Anchorage with a point extending several hundred yards towards Kolombangara in just such a position so as to put her under fire from the north, south and west. Her only escape lay through the door by which she had entered.

She noticed with pleasure how her big sisters kept the green and red tracers of their mighty guns lying continuously overhead. They looked like peaceful airplanes on their way, except for the crash and roar of their hits.

Maneuvering to get to her assigned station, a tremendous explosion rocked her in the water. A torpedo had hit one of her big sisters, the Strong. No submarine contact was ever made, however. Another sly Jap had slithered his way out of reach.

Her job was finished and the party was ready to go home. She took leave and left by the door in filial company. They formed a pretty parade as the sun peeked over the horizon, unaware of her and her sisters. He was very busy at his morning task of painting the clouds, the land and the sea.

She did not want to be caught close to the Jap airfield that morning, so she didn't stay to admire the sun's work. Instead she slipped into the first available mist and continued on her way, as oblivious of the Japanese hunting for her as she was of the seaweed on the bottom of the bay.

She scudded down the line and that night panted into the quiet lagoon at Port Purvis. Again she was happy, for she had twice, in approximately a month, slapped the protruding teeth of the enemy. The second time, she thought she could feel them give a little.

Her next two weeks were quietly spent recuperating from her two previous trips. Her heart quieted down a little. She made five or six routine trips with working ships to the north of her home. She twice slipped quietly up the Slot to deliver supplies to the fighting boys. She wanted to see how they were making out. She liked the way they were handling the situation and decided she wasn't needed there for a while. She began to get her breath again and got accustomed to jaunts. She was having the time of her life, punching the enemy where it hurt. She exulted in the knowledge that they would have given a lot just to know where she was.

At night, she could sometimes see anti-aircraft fire as she passed close to places the Japs thought she and her sisters were. The Japs were always mistaken.

She liked this little game of hide and seek. She knew if she played it right, she would walk without fear, either day or night, in places where she now crept stealthily through the dark.

On the 20th day of July, she found herself once more in the little bay she called home. She took a look around and decided that all was in order. The swaying palms were still standing straight and tall. The water of the bay looked so clean one imagined that if the light were right, all manner of sea things could be seen on its bottom. She took a deep breath and settled down for a good night's sleep.

She awoke once to firing at the curious Japs who were looking for her. A glance was all she needed, and she closed her eyes again and dropped off in her innocent sleep.

The next day she was busy once again. Early in the morning, she gathered with her sisters and they scrambled to Guadalcanal. They had work to do, and they were willing.

The girls waited eagerly for their dates and were not disappointed. Their friends came out to them well equipped to make merry on the following night.

They set out before dark on the expedition up past the Russells. She liked the crazy quilt pattern they made in the water. When they could see the flat-topped island marking the halfway point between Munda and her home, they swung eastward, then north as night closed in on them. Silently they glided over the phosphorescent sea, until the early hours of the morning. Before dawn broke, they slipped like giddy school girls into Kula Gulf.

They could see the evil cone of Kolombangara lurking to the north, swept clear of its clutches, and swung down past Rice Anchorage. The Lady sedately settled herself and hurried her boyfriends off to the beach as if sending them after a scoop of ice cream. (It was more like stealing apples…)

As before, her bigger sisters slugged the beach with their big guns. She liked the rumble overhead, and got the same thrill that comes with sitting under a trestle as a train is passing. Shells from the enemy batteries struck close, but, unbothered by the thought of getting hurt, she ignored them and was soon ready to go home. She must have led a charmed life.

She welcomed back one of the Dead-Enders she had forgotten on her previous trip and hied herself for home.

She reached Purvis Bay that evening, dug the latchkey from where she had it hidden, and let herself into the darkened seclusion. Exhausted, she slept.

The Japs slipped down by night to the place where she had been. By sly trickery they struck one of the cruisers that she had learned to call a friend. She heard the news the next day. Surprised and angry, she grieved for the Helena, but it was the price she must pay for playing such a dangerous game. Her grief was quickly covered with a sense of accomplishment. The third slap at the Jap was paying off. He too had lost ships that night, at Enogai, New Georgia. She intended to kick them off the islands for good and was making sure they knew it.

The next month was busy for her. She escorted men and equipment through the dangerous water to the north of Guadalcanal. She cavorted out past little Savo Island, stepping slightly around the slower fat LSTs. Though seemingly carefree, she was ever on alert for danger. Many times it came in the shape of "Shadowers" that would follow the formation for hours trying to get a likely target to bomb, strafe, or torpedo.

She took one little trip back up to the scene of her first party. The night was, as usual, dark - that black darkness she had come to call night in the Solomons.

Her job that night was to take some reinforcements to the little island of Oniavisi.

She liked her guests that night. They were just like her. These boys were big and quiet. They went about their work with the least amount of wasted motion. They were from Tonga Tabu. Born Jungle Fighters, they knew the jungle as you know the streets of the town you live in. Yes, she liked them. And besides, with their shoes slung over their shoulders, their bare feet tickled her back.

She took them to the little island and placed them on the beach. Out from there she strolled, cautious as always, feeling her way to the clear channel again.

She heard ships a little ways away, and called to them, but they did not answer. This startled her. Her friends always answered as she called to them. What was she to do? As near as she could tell, there were four of them, one awfully large, too. Maybe it was a cruiser. Should she hide and let them go on by? No, they might accidentally see her.

The ocean hissed and swirled around her feet and the wind hummed mightily in her hair as she flew through that narrow passage. Right behind her they came, closer and closer. She strained herself to the limit, and on they came. 6000, 5000, and still they closed on her. She was almost out of breath. Then just when she thought they must surely see or hear her, she felt the pressure of the chase lessen. They turned and made off on a new course.

She heaved a heavy sigh of relief, kept her speed awhile and then slowed down to a walk. It was a narrow escape and she felt more than a little shaky. It was the first time she had really been afraid.

Later she puzzled out the facts. The ruffians had been shelling the northwest corner of Rendova, and had decided to take a jaunt through Blanche Channel on their way home. Again she sighed a very grateful sigh and thanked God they hadn't seen her.

She stayed close to home, her nerves just a little shaky. After two weeks, she wasn't quite over the shock, but she was ready for the next job, and made it known.

She met her new guests off the white sandy beach of Guadalcanal on the 15th of August. She was to take them to Vella-la-Vella, as bait to trap the "Tokyo Express". The camp on the island was rumored to be a Japanese officers' rest camp. She knew this would be a good trick if she could do it.

By this time, the novelty of making the landings was wearing off. Each one was slightly different, but they all were constructed on the same plans.

She and her sisters sped quietly north. They passed Kilo Point, and saw the mute remains of the ships that the Japs had used to reinforce the bigger island of Guadalcanal in the early days. They were all that was left of a mighty force that had been completely destroyed by our aircraft.

Past Cape Esperence and Savo, and on past the Russells, she slipped into Blanche Channel between the now-friendly islands of Rendova and New Georgia. She slipped past the once powerful Jap airfield of Munda, and out into the unfriendly waters beyond, until she was off the island of Vella-la-Vella.

Day peeped over the pastel blue horizon, silhouetting the bulking form of Kolombangara. The Higgins children skittered across the remaining distance and slipped silently upon the sand. She had done it again. The thrill of a job well done rushed through her.

By this time it was broad daylight and time to leave. The trap was set and she could go home. She stretched herself as she started to move back down from Vella Gulf in the direction she had come from.

A few Jap planes lifted themselves off the side of Kolombungara, suspicious—then startled into full wakefulness when they spied the impudent little snips right in their front yard.

They wheeled for a moment, and were soon joined by several others. They pranced, feinted and then came to look over the lot. Perhaps they thought to finish the Lady and her friends then and there; to rid themselves of the dreaded little son-of-guns once and for all, that morning.

The Lady could have defended herself. Her bigger sisters, however, didn't intend to let the Japs get anywhere near her. They sped out on the offensive to meet the vultures as they winged close.

There was a sudden roar to break the silence and several harmless looking gray puffs in the midst of the group wheeling so serenely overhead. A couple of the planes fell off, trailing dark streamers as they went down. The rest were astounded at this show. They had never seen anything compare with the reaching that these tiny ships could do. More black puffs, more streamers. The formation broke up. This they were not ready to endure. They swung lower, clear down to the surface of the water, but each time their advance was blocked by these seemingly puny little ships.

At last they gave up and flew back to their eirie to lick their wounds. The Lady and her sisters pirouetted and left. Her fourth job was completed on August 15th 1943.

It was a well-set trap. The Japs lost a cruiser and four cans without any loss to us. We have some very gallant little cans to thank for that. The Admiral was well pleased with the way it all came out. So were we, and we knew the Lady was, too.

The rest of August, all of September and almost all of October raced by as the Lady worked. She was here one day, there the next; she visited her first landing places with pride as she entered their little bays and anchorages.

The lower Solomons no longer held terrors from beneath. She remembered every rock, reef and false channel. She'd been over them so many times she could have found her way blindfolded.

Sometimes in the evening, she would find herself in her favorite spot to watch the sun go down. The burning brightness would slowly sink to cool its incandescence in the sea. As it slid beneath the waves, the colors spread through the air and water. Red, blue, yellow and lavender would blend perfectly on the clouds. They were harsh at first, then they would pale with ever-changing designs, a pastel shade slowly changing into a billion stars as the night closed in.

She loved to watch all this from a point just off Koli, where Cape Esperence and Savo Island framed the origin of this tropical Aurora Borealis. Each one was different, but each was filled with a quiet splendor that put man and his "art" to shame.

The night would creep up with its silken mantle, and before she realized it, she was engulfed within its folds.

Far to the south she could make out the Southern Cross. Overhead was the Great Bear. She liked to see him. He had been with her through all her travels, and she regarded him as a friend. She couldn't see the North Star from where she was, but she could point to it at any time of the day or night. She was one with them. Someday maybe she would have a place among them as they wheeled endlessly overhead.

In the closing days of October, she became restless at the thought of the Jap getting so much peace and quiet in her relaxing efforts. It was time to remind them that she was still there and decidedly active.

She made an appointment with some boys who felt the same way. They were New Zealand boys and plenty tough. Veterans of the field. They would do nicely for the party she was planning.

She and her loyal sisters took the boys up north, this time to Treasury Islands just south of Bougainville. This would be her fifth direct action against the Japs.

The 27th of October, an uneventful trip took her within Higgins reach of Sterling Island. She hastened her boyfriends to the beach. This time the Jap was not caught flat-footed. He potted at the little boats with his mortars and rifles, but he could have sooner stopped the rising sun in its tracks. Soon it was quiet where the children played.

She returned to her home at Port Purvis and waited for a spell. On the 7th of November she put on her final dab of rouge and took a last look in the mirror to see if her skirts were straight. Then she snuk out with the girls for a gay time, to help the boys who had landed on the Island of Bougainville. The trip was rather uneventful. She dropped the boys, picked up some that had been hurt, and took them back to where they could get some aid.

Five days later, she heard they wanted more help, so she got ready to go again. They welcomed the boys and immediately went on their way. This trip seemed to be getting longer and longer. All night she steamed and well through the next day. Night fell and still they were going north. Chaperoning her fat sisters made for slow going, but Bougainville was calling and she was on her way with help.

The night before she arrived off Empress August Bay, she was kept on her toes by snooping Jap planes continuously following her group. But she didn't worry too much about them. They had done the same many times before. At these times, she was extra careful not to make a light or to keep too straight a course. If she did, it would all be over.

Suddenly a roar filled her ears. She jumped and looked around. A torpedo plane had almost crashed into her mast. She smiled a little then, but not for long. A sudden blaze reared its ugly head. The tin fish the torpedo plane had carried had hit one of her sisters. She blanched at the horrible sight. The ugly red glare turned the night into bloody day. For hundreds of feet into the air, flaming oil and exploding ammunition soared.

She called to her sister, but only a choked gurgling answered her. Her sister was dying. The other ships continued on as if nothing had happened, but the Lady wouldn't leave. She could help. She and a bigger sister stayed to see just how much.

The Dead-End-Kids were quickly put into the water, and sped to aid the men who lived within the Lady's sister. In ones and twos the men were clinging to one another and singing. Yes, they were singing as the little boats approached them. Simple little songs like Beer Barrel Polka. Some of them were hurt, and hurt badly; but still they sang.

Their captain claimed, "I'm alright, there's a couple of boys over there without lifejackets," but he was hoisted aboard despite his protests. He had been the last to leave his ship, and he was the first to be picked up.

The nosey Jap was still hanging around to see if he could do more damage, but the Lady and her big sister scared him off. After several attempts, he threw his last fish in a mad attempt to hit either of the little ships, but missed completely. It was getting light and the girls were beginning to place their shots uncomfortably close. Or maybe he was afraid his rice and fish were getting cold. Anyway, he left.

A small fire on the water marked the place where the McKean had gone down. It was the last thing proving she had even existed.

Her crew, pale and oil soaked, some of them bloody, were finally aboard the Lady. She cared for them as if they were her own. She had lost a friend she had loved dearly. Shaken and nervous, she left the grave.

She slipped into Empress Augusta Bay and her friends cheered her when she told them she had some of the boys from the McKean aboard.

The cheers were cut short, however, as a formation of Japanese planes appeared over the smoking volcano just east of the Bay. She was mad now, but she couldn't reach them. They dropped a few bombs that did no damage and went away. She ran her boys out on the beach and brought in the injured.

Her compassion for her human cargo knew no bounds. She put them in her little chambers and went south for Vella-la-Vella as hard as she could go.

On the way down, she heard that some Jap subs were waiting in Vella Gulf. She sidestepped them and took the boys on down to Guadalcanal. Tenderly she put them ashore and bade them goodbye and good luck. She stepped next door and let the boys from the McKean off at Tulagi, then came around Gavutu into her own little home for a much needed rest.

All during the Month of November she was on the go, but she was nervous. She was working too hard, so near the end of the month, the Admiral said she could take a rest.

Sydney, Australia was to be her resting place. She and her sisters wound their way to Noumea on their way down. As she left, she felt something give inside her. Something was wrong. She told the others to go without her; she had to go back into port.

The following month was spent at the hot little bay there at Noumea. It was a disappointing month. Three times she tried to get out, but each time she tried, the ache in her gizzard made her return.

The crew of the tender who worked on her did a good job, and she could finally go again – with a lingering difficulty backing up. But she wasn't the kind to back away from trouble. She'd be fine.

INTERLUDE AND MORE WORK

In Sydney, she whiled a quiet Christmas and New Years day. Her crew was having a good time. Of course it was the middle of summer there in the south and no snow or green and red Christmas decorations could be seen, but she was happy to be idle for a change.

She was sorry to leave Sydney, but she couldn't spend all her time there. Her crew would have been happy to stay a little longer too; but she wanted to go. So they came back to help her.

She made her way home to Purvis Bay by way of New Caledonia, the New Hebrides and Guadalcanal.

The month following Christmas was a very busy one, but not exciting. She called at some of the places she had been to renew acquaintances and exchange stories.

The 28th of January found her off Guadalcanal making another date. From there, she went on to Rice Anchorage and was off again. This time she was to take a survey party into the little island off the northern coast of Bougainville, up past the powerful Jap airfields on Buka. The Japs were thought to be using it as a stopover point for small boats bringing supplies down to their troops on Bougainville. It was almost exactly halfway between Rabaul and the other island. It was her job to go in with her boyfriends to see if this was being done.

At midnight the thirty-first of January she was off the little islet. Quietly she dropped the Dead-End-Kids in the water and they slid over to the island. She did not wait for them to come back, but hastened back towards Bougainville. She had a long way to go and was anxious to get away from the dangerous spot she was in.

All that day she wondered about the boys. But she couldn't find out anything except that they had been under air attack many times.

That night, she went back to pick them up and to find what they had learned. She was shocked to find that she had lost two of her boys in a sneak attack by the stealthy Jap. Two more of them were hurt and could barely make it back to her. She would take them where they could get the care they needed.

She had found out what she wanted to know. The Japs had taken the island and were using it as suspected. Our troops would have to take it away from the little devils.

She returned to her home and held a conference with the Admiral and Vice Admiral and all manner of big shots. It was finally decided that Green Island would be taken and she would have a part in it. She would have a chance to avenge her boys sleeping on foreign soil.

On February 14th, she was again off the little atoll. Her men worked her in the normal manner, and first thing she knew, the island was ours. The Japs had offered only slight interference. They wouldn't be using that little island for a base any more.

Almost three months passed before her next landing. By that time, she could have made her way in the new waters blindfolded.

The next little job took her up beyond New Ireland, the long narrow strip of land that lay just to the east of New Britain. The town of Kavieng lay on the northern end of it and was notorious for harboring Jap airplanes. But she was not to stop at New Ireland, and Kavieng passed in the night. She could see the lights of the airfield as she passed, but the Jap was busy with a slight case of battleship and cruiser trouble. They had no time to look for ships that would play their own tricks on them.

On the 22nd of April, she was off the beautiful little island of Emirau. The island was an incredible sight in the morning sun. She admired it form across a little strip of water.

For quite a little spell she lay there doing nothing. The native population gathered on the beach and watched history being made. Soon the little boats detached themselves from the ships and skittered across the world.

As they were passing a little islet on their way to beach, some wayward Japs opened fire on them. Their feeble attempts were quickly silenced, and soon the American flag flew on the beach and her seventh job was completed. She was happy again.

This was her last job in the Solomons and the Bismark Archipelago. During the months that she had been there, she had earned for her captain the Silver Star Medal, the Legion of Merit and the Bronze Star. She had made seven landings, with two of her men killed and four wounded. She had been very lucky, and was proud to know that she had done a fine job.

SHE HELPS MACARTHUR

Proudly she left Port Purvis on the morning of the 4th of April. Keeping a course almost due southwest, it wasn't very long before she had reached her destination.

General MacArthur had heard of the work the Lady and her friends had done, and wanted their help.

Her first port at New Guinea was Milne Bay. It stretched into the very interior of the goose-shaped island. Here she received her instructions.

She left the endless bay the 7th of April and beat her way northward to Cape Cretin. It was one like the others. She had long since learned that all these tropical stops would look the same, with the same deadly green trees and tepid waters. Oh, yes, the land would be shaped a little different and the beaches might be narrow or wide, white or black, but they all had the same feel.

At Cape Cretin she received her guests. They were bound for Aitape and she was to take them there. She left Cape Cretin the morning of April 24th and took to sneaking around the northwest tip of New Guinea. Her trip went smoothly.

The morning of the 26th found her at her destination. She proudly sailed into the wide-open bay. After she set her boys on the beach, she looked for targets, but could only find some insignificant tin shacks bordering the water. These she proceeded to manufacture into sieves. She was ready to leave in the early afternoon.

She was proud to know that she had been part of the largest amphibious movement that ever been undertaken in any part of the world. Aitape, Hollandia and another point away up on the western end of the island had all been taken. Almost 4000 ships had moved troops and ammunition over 600 miles to accomplish the job, and she'd played a role in it.

She went back to Cape Cretin and made a frantic hunt for some mail to make her men happy. She found none, despite her efforts, so the boys just moped around and grouched at each another.

She made another trip to Aitape, but all was quiet. The boys had done a good job. She wasn't needed in this area anymore, so she went back to Point Purvis until she could be called for another job.

Aitape was her eighth job and the honor of being a well-seasoned veteran weighed lightly on her. She was still a Lady.

After her return to Port Purvis, she was summoned for a new kind of work. She was to carry the boys who made it possible for the larger LST and LCI ships to land safely on the beaches. But that is another story.

ADVENTURE WITH DYNAMITE

She invited blow-up boys aboard and gave them rooms. She trained them in the difficult role of getting in and out of the water from her. After awhile they were very adept at this tricky maneuver. They became quite accomplished at slinging the heavy packs of high explosives around as they did their practice. She always felt rather uncomfortable while they did this, but she finally deemed herself ready for whatever job she should be assigned to do. She told her boss this and it wasn't long before he found one for her.

She said goodbye to her little home at Port Purvis on the morning of the 4th of June and, with some regret, she departed for Kwajalein.

Back across the equator she sped. Up north past Truk and Palau and a dozen other places that the Jap was still calling his own. Then on the morning of June the Eighth she entered the long, shell-like anchorage of Kwajalein.

There she greeted many old friends among the battleships and cruisers. Others were there too–brand new battleships, cruisers, carriers and many others. She liked the honest, hardworking appearance of these big new fellows and felt she could count on them from the word go.

She was here to help recover the Mariannas base of Guam. She liked that. She felt a little giddy about it all, though a little unsure of herself in so big a job, but as usual, she was game. She left Kwajalein the 10th of June, found a place in the big parade and started her trip.

That night she dozed off. She wasn't listening and consequently she wasn't where she should have been at the time she should have been there.

A dark shape loomed, covering the horizon. It bore down on her with all the grace of a juggernaut and struck her a nasty blow right on the nose. Stunned, she barely managed to get out of the way before someone else ran her over. She got back in her place and called the admiral to tell him what had happened. He told her to go back to Eniwetok and get her bridgework back in shape.

She did, and was ready to go again in less than 24 hours, but she wasn't completely fixed. She ached and groaned in every joint. Her old injury from Noumea still hurt. She went on though, determined to carry out her job.

All alone, she crossed the forbidding wastes that lay between Eniwetoc and Saipan, finally making her stand the morning she was originally supposed to be there.

She gaped at the beautiful sights that met her gaze. They reminded her of the home she had left far across the sea. In the barren hills she saw the lands around the Golden Gate. On Tinian, across the narrow straight, she saw the green, fertile, grassy meadows of the lands up the bay from San Francisco. She liked it and was glad that they were destined to be part of her homeland.

Her big friends wielded tremendous power that day, on the shores of these enemy bastions. The numerous incidents she witnessed are too many to mention.

She smiled at the sight of a battleship the Japs had put to the bottom of Pearl Harbor, as it lay between the two islands, blazing away at targets on both shores. It was a just reward for the sneaking little heathens.

She was amazed to see the whole side of a rocky

promontory topple and crash into the sea. Cruisers had set off an ammunition dump that supplied the firepower for the emplacements there.

Anxious, she set off with some of her bigger sisters toward duties in Guam, but frantic words turned her on her heels. It would be suicide to go any closer. Many shore batteries had been spotted that would have made her less than a sieve in even less time than it takes to tell. It was just a little too much for her to handle. She would wait until the other girls could help her, after they had finished the little job at Saipan.

For a few days, she was at Saipan leaning heavily on her anchor chain in the little bay. She got a real kick watching the progress of the boys ashore.

She was thrilled to watch a duel between a destroyer and an impudent shore battery. The destroyer had suffered at the hands of the Japs at Pearl Harbor.

The little ship was working its way up the bay close inshore when the Jap opened up on her. She heeled about and dashed madly for safety. The Jap could almost be heard cursing at his own poor aim.

Another little ship was working its way into the same position and had been hit by this gun. She lay beside another vessel made to take care of cases like this.

The destroyer ignored the fact that she was motionless as the men worked day and night to help her. She busily fired her big guns until the battery was out of action. She enthusiastically worked almost every threat she could see over to a fair-the-well. This was almost amusing. She smiled at the sight. Nothing could beat these boys and girls once they got started.

After several days of watching the big battle, and several nights dodging sneaking bombs that straddled her and bounced her at her anchorage, she lost her front seat at the show. She transferred her boys to another ship. She was sorry to see them go, as she had made many friends among them.

On Independence Day in 1944, she took her orders in her hand and left Saipan on her way to Pearl Harbor.

She arrived in Pearl Harbor with a wish in her heart. She had spent 17 months in the tropics, working her heart out. Her insides were hurting her badly and she ached and pained in every joint. She was ready to have a time in the hospital. The rest-cure would work wonders with her.

She stood listlessly along the Destroyer Escort Docks in Pearl Harbor as she waited for the Admiral to grant her wish. He did, and she left for San Francisco.

The 11th of July found her entering the Bay. She wondered anew at the flimsy looking bridge spanning the Gate. But this had been seen before, and she was tired.

She quickly slipped in among the docks and piers along the waterfront. A little while later, she sent her crew home on leave. Then she went to sleep.

After she had gone to sleep, and her crew had parted to places best known only to them, she was operated on.

They worked on her inwards and outwards until she shone with all the brilliance that had punctuated her work.

She was home for only six weeks, but the call was strong within her. She became restless again to go, and facing the inevitable, she said she was ready.

THE LAST ADVENTURE????

After being out again, the feeling died down in her sturdy little heart. Once more she was one with the sea and the wind.

Her first little jaunt ended at Pearl Harbor. Nosing her slight frame through the net, she nestled down with a couple of newcomers: ladies like herself who were out to do the same job. They were inquisitive, but the Lady did not talk much. She answered their questions, but did not volunteer any information.

She had to run down to Maui before she went on out, after some more boyfriends. These friends of hers always seemed to be pretty fast company, so were ready when she said she wanted to go to the Philippines.

It was going to be a long hard trip across the Pacific, so back to Pearl Harbor she went to pack her bags and get ready to go.

From Pearl, she found the path to Eniwetoc, took only a breath there and thence on to Manus Island. She had passed the Admiralties on her way to Aitape a half a year before. She did not venture close that time, because the Nips still held it with some force. It was not until some months later while she was at the job at Emirau that Mac

Arthur's men were to chase the Little Yellow Men back into the sea.

Now, the bay was loaded with more big sisters and friends than she had seen in a long, long time. She seemed happy to make new friends and to renew old ones. It really looked like a good show later on, so she decided to run along with them.

It wasn't long before they were getting ready to leave. She grabbed her hat and coat and set off with them.

The trip from Manus to the little island of Leyte was further enhanced by a typhoon, but she was an old salt from way back. She joked and danced with him until he was tired, then he staggered home. She was still fresh as a daisy.

The ruffians were trying to trick the Lady in the corridor, so she and her friends decided to wait for the time being. Soon they were removed and the party was ready to start.

It was three days before the rest of the folks would be around, and they wouldn't like the old trees, machine gun nests and other odds and ends kicking around the place. Time to tidy up the scenery. Her boyfriends helped out by digging around the water's edge.

The Nips weren't like the girls. They rather liked the scenery just the way it was. She was tired and rather worn when they had finally cleaned up their share of the work. Anyway, the others would have lots more cleaning gear when they arrived. They would finish dusting off the place then. They whiled away the hours with idle chatter and a few practice dance steps.

Company came, with a great deal of chatter, a couple days later and finished the job. Amusingly, the Japs put out from Tokyo about being everything from sunk to pushed back with only half her men.

She had never been on a wild party like this before. Her parties had always been respectable, but this was a real bang up to remember for a long time. Since she had finished her job a short time after her arrival, she edged close for a good look at the activity. There were several of her old chums whose names started with B, and also lots of the others. They were very energetic and eager with their work.

She watched the symphony as it started with solos from her biggest friends. Then as they progressed their way through the score, the others joined them. Soon the whole world seemed to resound at the cacophony of their efforts. Then just before the efforts of their boyfriends, the earth trembled at the deafening climax of the score. It was almost impossible for her mind to keep up with the complicated rhythm that continued for the breath-taking eternity of almost a quarter of an hour.

Then silence; punctuated with the symbol clashes of her soloist friends who had started it all. It was very impressive. She thought that it had impressed the Japs even more than it had her.

From the 18th of October to the afternoon of the 21st she lazed around in Leyte Gulf, until she'd had enough. Her boyfriends and some other companions thought it was time to go too, so back to Manus they started.

Almost from the time she left, she began to hear that rowdy bunch she had been with were at it again. She kept her ear peeled for evidence of the fun they were having, but her nose pointed steadily away. She had found the company was a little fast. This party would be remembered for a long time, as it was officially called "The Second Battle of the Philippines."

She dropped her boyfriends after she got there at Manus, and rested in the tepid waters at the now deserted bay. She was there for almost a month before her wanderlust was at it again. She strolled over to Oro Bay to see some old friends, then took the mail to Cape Gloucester, on the island of New Britain. She had operated far to the other side of the island and had often seen it, but this was the first time she had ever touched on its shores.

She admired the little bay that looked so much like her old home at Purvis. The volcano was scrutinized closely from a respectable distance. The she wandered off to Manus for more dozing in the warm bath treatment.

She was dozing quietly in the warm water, when she was very rudely awakened. A tremendous shock shook her frail frame and nearly rolled her over. Almost immediately she lost consciousness.

She awoke to find she had received numerous wounds. Great gaping gashes rent her tender skin, and deep inside were more hurts. Her first concern was her crew, but only a few showed minor scratches. That relieved her somewhat, but whence had come this horrible catastrophe?

She looked around. A pillar of smoke about 800 yards from her mercifully shielded the tragedy from her gaze. The ammunition ship was gone. It had exploded. She had often warned the others not to play with fire, and now these poor boys had paid the price of this terrible accident.

She was hurting. Aid must come and fast. She crawled up the bay to the first aid station and was quickly bandaged, but she would carry the scars for the rest of her life.

After a short convalescence, she could navigate once more.

This land of strange names intrigued her, and she was ready to leave this harbor that had almost been the scene of her death. So on the 15th of December she took leave and spent

[Editor's note: pages 48 and 49 of the typewritten copy that this was transcribed from were missing at the time of publication.]

Back to Subic Bay. On the 17th of January, she picked up some parachutists who had passed over the island early that morning. She raced at full speed. With the children

Higgins, she dropped the boys off on the white sandy beach at the foot of the big rock. She felt highly pleased. From now on the bay behind Corrigador would be free and open to the people of the Navy.

From here on out, the Japs would be losing their own land, and finally paying for their treachery. She was very proud of the work she had done, from the quiet waters of San Diego to this spot halfway around the world.

She scuffed the highways of the sea she loved, going to Ulithi, Manus, and Guam, for the first time since her party there.

She took a stroll one day to another place that will have to remain nameless for the time. But nothing exciting took place there, so she doesn't seem to mind my not mentioning it.

She slipped back to Guam and then to Ulithi, where the Admiral had a bit of a job for her.

"Yes, she would rather volunteer to go." No, there were no objections and she could find her way. Just give her a guidebook and she could find her way anyplace now.

She followed the chart and found herself at Okinawa. This was April 26th 1945. She explored for a couple of days and dodged the usual Jap air attacks, then slipped back to Saipan.

Off the very beach where she had watched so much war and destruction only a few months previously, she watched the great wings of the giant bombers that used this as a home. She felt akin to the slowly moving giants, who day-by-day mysteriously slipped into the north. They were doing their bit kicking the Japanese in the teeth, continuing the job she had joined in so long before.

She heard that she was going to be retired to a less active life. Somehow it didn't sound as bad as it had 3 years before. She had some rest coming to her, and she dared to hope (but not too much) that it would take her home.

She took another trip to Okinawa, from May 22nd to

June 6th - the third anniversary of her baptism by fire at Dutch Harbor. The knowledge that Jap planes were on their way didn't thrill her the way it used to.

Occasionally one would get too close, and once more the old feeling would surge through her. The excitement took its toll though, and she heaved and trembled after it was over. She would tremble for hours after they had left. She was just getting too old, and she knew it.

She left Okinawa with a happy heart but a tired body. The boys could carry on the old tradition she'd set up. She knew she was leaving the future in good hands.

She dropped into Saipan and was relieved by the Admiral. He told her to go to Eniwetoc and from there to Pearl.

This story ends here. Who knows what will to happen to her in the future. Her deeds have made the newspaper headlines all over the world. True, she was never named, but she is happy to know that whenever anyone speaks of Rendova, Munda, Bougainville, Aitape, Corrigador, The Philippines Invasion, and many more; they are unconsciously praising her. There is not one man aboard her who does not admire her record and the life she has led. In case you are interested, here is the condensed form of the facts that have previously been mentioned:

She has sailed around the world more than 6 times, if her trips were laid end to end. She has crossed the equator 8 times, and the Pacific Ocean 6. She has consumed a couple million gallons of fuel in her escapades, and literally tons of food has fueled her men.

She has sailed some one hundred and thirty or more missions against the Japs, and made them unhappy with at least 16 that were either first assaults or close support landings. Many of them were with only her small sisters in company and support, striking like a snake, without warning and apparently without reason or rhyme to the enemy—but the results have been proven.

Her captain wears, in addition to campaign bars for duty in three areas in the Pacific, some 8 stars for direct action in a recognized campaign or battle. He also can thank her directly for the three medals that he wears, namely: The Silver Star, the Bronze Star, and the Legion of Merit. She numbers in her crew, winners of two Silver Stars, 1 bronze star, and 6 purple hearts of which 3 of the purple hearts were awarded posthumously.

A final word on her behalf. A toast, by Lt. Gen. Simon Buckner, "may you walk on the ashes of Tokyo."

Follows is a list of the ports that she has hit since the start of the war.

Port	Approximate date of arrival and departure.
San Diego, Calif.	Dec 7, 1941
Pearl Harbor, T.H.	Dec 14, 1941
San Francisco, Calif.	Dec 30, 1941
San Diego, Calif.	Jan 1, 1942
San Francisco, Calif.	Feb-Mar-Apr, 1942
Bremerton, Wash.	Feb, 1942
Seattle, Wash.	Mar 25, 1942
Dutch Harbor, Als.	June 2, 1942
Makushin Bay, Unalaska I.	June 3, 1942
Dutch Harbor, Unalaska I.	June 11, 1942
Kodiak Island	June 23, 1942
Anchorage, Als.	June 25, 1942

Kodiak, Als.	June 31, 1942
Seward, Als.	July 2, 1942
Dutch Harbor, Als.	July 6, 1942
Nome, Als.	July 9, 1942
Dutch Harbor, Als.	July 18, 1942
Chernofski Bay, Unalaska I.	July 22, 1942
Dutch Harbor, Als.	July 25, 1942
Seattle, Wash.	Aug 1, 1942
Dutch Harbor, Als.	Aug 26, 1942
Adak, Andreanoff Is. Gr. Als.	Sept 1, 1942 (assault)
Dutch Harbor, Als.	Sept 3, 1942
Seattle, Wash.	Sept 12, 1942
Dutch Harbor, Als.	Oct 8, 1942
Seattle, Wash.	Oct 16, 1942
Kodiak, Als.	Oct 25, 1942
Sand Point, Als.	Oct 28, 1942
Dutch Harbor, Als.	Oct 29, 1942
Adak, Als.	Nov 3, 1942
Atka, Als.	Nov 8, 1942
Dutch Harbor, Als.	Nov 14, 1942
Chernofski Bay, Als.	Nov 15, 1942
Nazan Bay, Atka, Als.	Nov 17, 1942
Dutch Harbor, Als.	Nov 23, 1942

Kodiak, Als.	Nov 26, 1942
Adak, Als.	Dec 8, 1942
Dutch Harbor, Als.	Dec 20, 1942
Adak, Als.	Dec 30, 1942
Dutch Harbor	Jan ??, 1943
Amchitka, Als.	Jan 30, 1943 (assault reinforcement)
San Francisco, Calif.	Feb 6, 1943
Mare Island, Calif.	Feb 6, 1943
----------------------------	----------------------------
Left U.S.A. for duty sopac.	Mar 16, 1943
Pearl Harbor, T.H.	Mar 23, 1943
Espiritu, Santo, New Heb.	Apr 3, 1943
Noumea, New Caledonia	Apr 27, 1943
Tonga Tabu, Kingdom	May 27, 1943
Noumea, New Caledonia	May ??, 1943
Townsville, N.Q. Aust.	May 17, 1943
Noumea, New Caledonia	June 30, 1943
Guadalcanal, Sols.	June 2-4, 1943
Noumea, New Caledonia	June 7-10, 1943
Auckland, N.Z.	June 14-16, 1943
Noumea, New Caledonia	June 19-20, 1943
Guadalcanal, Sols.	June 24-26, 1943
Port Purvis, Florida Is. Sols.	June 26-28, 1943

Guadalcanal	June 28, 1943
Russell Islands	June 29, 1943
Oniavisi, New Georgia Gr.	June 30, 1943 (assault)
Guadalcanal	July 1-2, 1943
Rice Anchorage, New Georgia	July 4-5, 1943
Purvis Bay	July 5-3, 1943
Rendova, New Georgia Gr.	July 9, 1943
Guadalcanal	July 10, 1943
Purvis Bay	July 11-15, 1943
Russell Islands	July 16, 1943
Rendova	July 17, 1943
Purvis Bay	July 18-19, 1943
Rendova	July 20, 1943
Guadalcanal	July 23, 1943
Enogai, New Georgia, Sols.	July 24, 1943 (assault)
Purvis Bay	July 25-26, 1943
Rendova	July 26-27, 1943
Purvis Bay	July 28-30, 1943
Guadalcanal	July 30, 1943
Oniavisi	July 31, 1943
Guadalcanal	Aug 1, 1943

Purvis Bay	Aug 1-6, 1943
Guadalcanal	Aug 6-8, 1943
Purvis Bay	Aug 8-12, 1943
Guadalcanal	Aug 12-14, 1943
Vella-la-Vella, Nor. Sols.	Aug 15, 1943 (assault)
Purvis Bay	Aug 15-24, 1943
Guadalcanal	Aug 24, 1943
Rice Anchorage	Aug 26, 1943
Purvis Bay	Aug 26-29, 1943
Guadalcanal	Aug 29, 1943
Enogai	Aug 29-30, 1943
Purvis Bay	Aug 30-Sept 4, 1943
Rendova	Sept 5, 1943
Purvis Bay	Sept 6-10, 1943
Munda Bar	Sept 10, 1943
Purvis Bay	Sept 11-16, 1943
Guadalcanal	Sept 16-17, 1943
Vella-la-Vella	Sept 17, 1943
Purvis Bay	Sept 13-23, 1943
Guadalcanal	Sept 25, 1943
Vella-la-Vella	Sept 25-26, 1943
Purvis Bay	Sept 26-Oct 9, 1943
Guadalcanal	Oct 10, 1943

Munda Bar	Oct 10, 1943
Purvis Bay	Oct 11-13, 1943
Guadalcanal	Oct 13-14, 1943
Munda Bar	Oct 19-20, 1943
Purvis Bay	Oct 21-26, 1943
Treasury Islands Gr.	October 27, 1943 (assault)
Purvis Bay	Oct 28-Nov 4, 1943
Guadalcanal	Nov 4, 1943
Bougainville	Nov 6, 1943
Guadalcanal	Nov 8, 1943
Purvis Bay	Nov 8-9, 1943
Guadalcanal	Nov 9, 1943
Bougainville	Nov 11, 1943 (assault support)
Guadalcanal	Nov 12, 1943
Purvis Bay	Nov 12-15, 1943
Guadalcanal	Nov 15, 1943
Bougainville	Nov 17, 1943
Guadalcanal	Nov 18, 1943
Purvis	Nov 18-23, 1943
Guadalcanal	Nov 21, 1943
Noumea	Nov 24-Dec 20, 1943
Sydney, N.S.W. Aust.	Dec 23-Jan 2, 1944

Noumea	Jan 5-8, 1944
Espiritu Santos	Jan 9-10, 1944
Guadalcanal	Jan 13, 1944
Purvis Bay	Jan 13, 1944??
Guadalcanal	Jan 13-15, 1944
Russell Islands	Jan 15, 1944
Purvis Bay	Jan15-16, 1944
Rendova	Jan 17, 1944
Treasury Islands Group	Jan 20-21, 1944
Purvis Bay	Jan 22-26, 1944
Guadalcanal	Jan 26, 1944
Russell Islands	Jan 26, 1944
Purvis Bay	Jan 26-28, 1944
Guadalcanal	Jan 28, 1944
Rice Anchorage	Jan 29-30, 1944
Green Island	Jan 31, 1944 (survey)
Vella-la-Vella	Feb 1, 1944
Green Island	Feb 1, 1944 (survey retrieve)
Guadalcanal	Feb 3, 1944
Purvis Bay	Feb 3-13, 1944
Guadalcanal	Feb 13, 1944
Vella-la-Vella	Feb 14, 1944
Green Island	Feb 15, 1944

	(assault)
Purvis Bay	Feb 16-17, 1944
Guadalcanal	Feb 17, 1944
Green Island	Feb 19, 1944
Purvis Bay	Feb 20-22, 1944
Russell Islands	Feb 22-Mar 1, 1944
Purvis Bay	Mar 1-7, 1944
Guadalcanal	Mar 7-8, 1944
Purvis Bay	Mar 8-9, 1944
Guadalcanal	Mar 10, 1944
Russell Islands	Mar 11, 1944
Hawthorne Sound, Rendova	Mar 14, 1944
Purvis Bay	Mar 15-17, 1944
Russell Islands	Mar 17, 1944
Emirau Is., Bismark Arch.	Mar 20, 1944 (assault)
Purvis Bay	Mar 23-Apr 4, 1944
Milne Bay, New Guinea	Apr 6-7, 1944
Cape Cretin, New Guinea	Apr 8-18, 1944
Aitape, New Guinea	Apr 22, 1944 (assault)
Cape Cretin	Apr 23-24, 1944
Aitape	Apr 26, 1944 (assault support)

Cape Sudest, New Guinea	Apr 26-30, 1944
Cape Cretin	May 1, 1944
Aitape	May 4-5, 1944
Cape Sudest	May 7-9, 1944
Purvis Bay	May 13-18, 1944
Guadalcanal	May 18-21, 1944
Purvis Bay	May 21-24, 1944
Guadalcanal	May 24-26, 1944
Purvis Bay	May 26-Jun 4, 1944
Kwajalien, Marshall Is.	June 8-10, 1944
Eniwetoc, Marshall Atoll	June 11-12, 1944
Saipan, Mariannas Is.	June 16, 1944 (assault)
Guam, Mariannas Is.	June 17, 1944 (attempted assault)
Saipan	June 18-23, 1944
Pearl Harbor	July 3-4, 1944
San Francisco, Calif.	July 11-Aug 28, 1944
Pearl Harbor	Sept 3-12, 1944
Maui, T.H.	Sept 12-14, 1944
Pearl Harbor	Sept 14-15, 1944
Eniwetoc	Sept 25-28, 1944
Manus, Admiralty Is. N.G.	Oct 3-12, 1944
Leyte, Philippine Is.	Oct 18-22, 1944

	(assault)
Manus	Oct 27-Nov 2, 1944
Oro Bay, New Guinea	Nov 4-5, 1944
Cape Glouchester, N.Br.	Nov 6-7, 1944
Manus	Nov 7-Dec 15, 1944
Noemfoor, Dutch East Indies	Dec 18-25, 1944
Mios Woendi, D.E.I.	Dec 26-28, 1944
Noemfoor	Dec 29-Jan 1, 1945
Biak, D.E.I.	Jan 1, 1945
Japen, D.E.I.	Jan 2, 1945
Noemfoor	Jan 3-4, 1945
Lingayen	Jan 11-12, 1945
San Pedro Bay, Leyte, P.I.	Jan 16-27, 1945
Nasugbu, Luzon, P.I.	Jan 31, 1945 (assault)
San Jose, Mindoro I., P.I.	Feb 1-3, 1945
San Pedro	Feb 6-7, 1945
Mangarin Bay, Leyte	Feb 8-9, 1945
Subic Bay, Luzon, P.I.	Feb 10-14, 1945
Mariveles, Luzon, P.I.	Feb 15, 1945 (assault)
Subic Bay	Feb 15, 1945
Corrigador, Luzon, P.I.	Feb 17, 1945 (assault)

Subic Bay	Feb 17, 1945
San Pedro Bay	Feb 25, 1945
Ulithi Atoll	Mar 1-23, 1945
Manus	Mar 26-27, 1945
Ulithi Atoll	Mar 30- Apr 1, 1945
Guam	April 2-4, 1945
(censored)	April 7-13, 1945
Guam	April 16-19, 1945
Ulithi	April 20-21, 1945
Okinawa, Ryukyu's Gr.	April 26-30, 1945
Saipan	May 5-18, 1945
Okinawa	May 28-June 6, 1945
Saipan	May 12-14, 1945
Eniwetoc	May 17-18, 1945
Pearl Harbor	May 25---------

"Finis"

EPILOGUE

It was July that welcomed her in. Yes, she had come home. She had made the crossing from Pearl to San Pedro safely and uneventfully. Her crew knew she was quite interested in reaching home, to bring her charges back to the land they had left with such heavy hearts, and to keep the promise she had made to herself on those eventful days so long before.

She was still almost 300 miles away when her super-eyes glimpsed the coast through the darkness and fog. She gave a quiet sigh as she stepped along her path.

It was only a couple days later that she allowed herself to be stripped of her deadly cargo. Placidly she lay as she knew she would never again feel the assurance of one who was not only willing to fight but also ready and quite capable.

The next day she proudly stepped up the little path that would shelter her for a while.

It was at this time I left her for a few days of rest, to go home—home, after being with such a glamorous lady. But she knew her faults, and made no protest.

I came back to her after a month had passed. She was as a very old lady now. Steeped into her almost-living metal was the dignity that no one could destroy, despite the disfigurations that had occurred during my absence.

Though lying in her deathbed, she was alert. For as an old lady, she had been ever glued to the "Party line" that would bring her news of this new fangled "A-BOMB" and its results.

Then came the quiet, matter-of-fact announcement: "War Ends" given by her Commander in Chief, President Truman, on August 15, 1945.

She exulted in the knowledge that she and her kind had helped to bring it about. She also knew that a new era had opened and that she was now just an "old fashioned lady." She lapsed into the coma of the utterly weary.

I left her just a few days later. I left her with no small amount of cotton wadding in my throat. I didn't look back at her as I walked down the dock - I couldn't. But she knew I couldn't and gave me her blessing as I left.

It was later in October I received word that she was now among the many who paid the highest price in the service of her country.

She's gone now. But her memory will live on in the hearts of the men who served with her.

Her passing opens a new and glorious future. But it is for the many who were fortunate to work with her that I speak. Place a simple marker on some windy ocean swept beach and on it inscribe the following:

U.S.S. Talbot (D114)(APD7)
Born: World War I (1918)
Died: World War II (1945)
Rest In Peace
A Lady to the End.

ABOUT THE AUTHOR

Ellis Holden Kinyon was born in 1921 and grew up in Montesano, Washington. He went by "Kinny".

"My first sight of her was in the quiet year of 1941 and the even quieter year of May."

He served aboard the USS Talbot DD114/APD-7 before and during World War II in the Pacific, as Radioman Third Class, and eventually Radioman First Class.

After the war, he was promoted to Chief and became a husband and a father.

He was lost in a sailing accident in 1958.

The Odyssey Of A Lady

The Odyssey Of A Lady describes real events that occurred during World War II.

To learn more about the historical context of the story, about how this book came to be, and about the author, Ellis Holden Kinyon, visit the accompanying website:

http://the-odyssey-of-a-lady.tumblr.com/